UNIVERSITY OF NORTH CAROLINA
STUDIES IN THE ROMANCE LANGUAGES
AND LITERATURES

A New Interpretation of Chrétien's
Conte Del Graal

Urban T. Holmes, Jr.

CHAPEL HILL

NUMBER EIGHT   1948

Copyright, 1948
THE UNIVERSITY OF NORTH CAROLINA

STUDIES IN THE ROMANCE
LANGUAGES AND LITERATURES

FOREWORD

It is now just ten months since I published in *Studies in Philology* XLIV (1947), No. 3 (July), 453-476, the article which is reprinted herewith. During this interval I have received many letters, a few expressing disagreement, and a considerable number indicating a tendency to agree. Those who have long upheld the Celtic origins theory use the argument with me that theirs can be the only correct solution because it is proved beyond question. They commend my industry, and ingenuity, but see no reason to look for parallels in other literary, folk, and ritual traditions. They say that I have not read their books and articles closely enough.

Anticipating further criticism, and this time in print, I am hoping that our opponents will not make use of the "one swallow" technique of refutation. With apologies to John Heywood for parodying his "One swallow maketh not summer" I have in mind that kind of refutation where an occasional occurrence of a parallel elsewhere, in other traditions, is cited to cast doubt upon a rather heavy concentration of facts in an argument. The *argumentum ex silentio* may be brought in at this point to multiply the stray swallow into a whole migration; but the maintenance of an essential *sens* throughout a mediaeval work can not be inferred from a few disparate and scattered parallels. Because a Christian Biblical scholar in the eleventh or twelfth century may have said something similar to what we believe Chrétien de Troyes drew from the Midrash, does not prove that Chrétien was not originally a Jew nor does it deny our whole Judaeo-Christian theory and attribute the structure of the *Conte del Graal* to a Celtic fantasy.

Another line of refutation, which we trust will not be used by our opponents, is that which asserts that "the whole is no better than the tiniest of its parts." If we have slipped in some detail there should be no inference that we have skidded with our whole structure. I have in mind one case in point. We owe to A. H. Schutz the reference about the questions at the Passover feast (see our p. 21). When our theory first appeared in print Professor Schutz noted that the form of questioning which we gave was slightly inaccurate. This is now revised. Such a slip as this should have no bearing upon the validity of our theory.

I have recently been informed that a group of European scholars are preparing a cooperative volume in which they also will seek to prove Oriental origins (presumably Manichaean) for the story of the Grail. We should welcome all efforts to arrive at the truth in this most important field of research. I am reprinting the present study because many colleagues have asked for offprints and I have long ago distributed the few that were at my disposal.

I wish to thank the editorial board of *Studies in Philology* for their permission to reprint this material.

Chapel Hill, May 6, 1948. U. T. H.

A NEW INTERPRETATION OF CHRÉTIEN'S *CONTE DEL GRAAL*

The present writer is tremendously aware of the vast amount of material that has been written to explain the symbols and the origin of the Holy Grail.[1] The three principal theories are (1) that the Grail procession and the facts attendant upon it are derived from the Christian Sacrifice of the Mass, perhaps from the Byzantine rite; (2) that the Grail story combines a group of more or less related Celtic tales, with perhaps some additional elements thrown in; (3) that the Grail is reminiscent of a fertility cult, such as that of Adonis or the Eleusinian Mysteries. James Douglas Bruce, Konrad Burdach, and Rose Peebles have made prominent contribution towards the Christian explanation; the late A. C. L. Brown, and more recently, William A. Nitze, and Helen Adolf, have argued strongly for the Celtic; Miss Jessie L. Weston will always be remembered for her critique of the other theories and insistence upon cultist origins. The earlier writings on the Grail are summarized effectively by James Douglas Bruce in his *The Evolution of Arthurian Romance* (Göttingen, 1927, 2nd ed.). Very recently indeed Nitze and Miss Adolf have taken up the problem, once more. Nitze observed in *MLN*, XIX (1944), 567:

> The time is ripe for some Romance scholar to collaborate with a Celticist in a book on Chrétien's last romance.

In *Speculum*, XXI (July, 1946), 303-311, Nitze undertakes to do some of this. He believes that one of the source tales told how Perceval had to recover a fertility cup for his clan (against the Red Knight); still another was concerned with a cauldron of plenty which had some connection with the Fisher King (Irish Nuadu). To elaborate upon this vessel and "place it in the brightest light" it was identified with a *graal*, reminiscent of the Byzantine Mass. The bleeding lance was a Gawain story, but it and the Grail procession are reminiscent of the Byzantine rite. In sum, Chrétien "in true mediaeval fashion . . . modern-

---

[1] This attempt at a new interpretation of the Grail episode in Chrétien has been in part a cooperative effort in which my colleagues Alfred Engstrom and Robert W. Linker have given invaluable counsel.

ized antiquity . . . . So he would place Celtic legend (his chief source), Byzantine ritual, the lance of Longinus, Good Friday penitence, Alexander—all on the same evangelical level." His mainstay in this was Philip of Flanders.

Miss Helen Adolf also, in *Modern Language Quarterly*, VIII (March, 1947), 3-19, seeks to carry out Professor Nitze's instructions in much the same way, but she gives different details. For her the Grail (or cup) carried by the fairy equals a fairy. The Fisher King is, as Brown had previously suggested, death-in-life; the bleeding lance stands for a wounded man; and so on. She makes this general statement:

> Our theory, however, would rest on a weak foundation, if it were not supported by the fact that there are plenty of inconsistencies in Chrétien's romance. These point to a multiplicity of defective joints and transitions (p. 7).

Personally I am fearful of our creating more inconsistencies than any mediaeval man ever dreamed of by this redoubled effort to explain the *Contes del Graal* of Chrétien as a monstrous combine of Celtic tale, fairy lore, Byzantine Mass, metonymy, and mistakes. I should like to make another effort, following different lines of thought, to seek a more consistent solution. In doing this we will assume that the original meaning of the Grail was not known to the continuators of Chrétien or to those who wrote other Grail works. Thus we will exclude from our investigation the *Perlesvaus*, Robert of Boron, Wolfram von Eschenbach and the prose Vulgate Cycle, which are quite frequently cited by Grail scholars, who thereby give the impression that they think these later writers had some acquaintance with Chrétien's sources. With that we do not agree.

For the reader's benefit we will review very briefly the significant motifs of the Grail Castle and procession as presented by Chrétien in his *Perceval*.

Perceval is seeking a place to lodge and he comes upon a river. He sees a boat with two men fishing, using for bait little fish slightly larger than minnows. One of the men directs him to a castle which he finds with some difficulty. As he gazes upon it he thinks it fairer than anything from there to Beyruth. He enters over the drawbridge; four servitors appear and he is wrapped in a mantle of scarlet. (This need not mean "vermeille," but it usually does.) He finds a series of *loges* leading to a great hall, perfectly square, in which there are columns of copper. An old man is in the center by a fire, clad in black with purple edging.[2] Four hundred men could have been contained in that hall. Perceval sits with the old man upon his couch. A squire enters with a sword, sent by the old man's *nièce, la sore pucele*, to be given to anyone whom he may choose. The sword is handed to Perceval, for whom it has been destined. It is remarked that there are only three of its kind and that there will be no more; furthermore that it will fail its possessor in only one case known to the maker.[3] Next comes the Grail procession. A squire enters with a lance that drops blood on the bearer's hand. Two more squires appear with ten branched candlesticks and then a damsel with a Grail in her hand. There is bright light around the Grail. They are followed by a second damsel with a silver plate. Perceval asks no questions and the procession goes out. An ivory table is brought and placed upon trestles of strange and rare wood. The meat is a venison haunch. The food is served to each upon a "gastel qui fu antiers." At each course the damsel with the Grail returns and passes between the couch and the fire. Perceval puts off all questions until the morrow. That evening he is served many delicious fruits *au couchier*. When the day dawns the Castle appears deserted. Perceval finds his arms and goes forth. The drawbridge pulls up after him. He soon encounters a girl holding the headless trunk of a knight who was recently killed in fight. She asks Perceval whether he had spent the night at the Castle of the "rice roi Pecheor." He says yes. She tells him that the host and the fisher were the same, that the king had been wounded in a battle, in both *hanches*, and that if he had asked concerning the Castle and the procession "Le buen roi qui est maheigniez, Toz eüst ragaeigniez Ses manbres

> D'un sebelin noir come more,
> A une porpre vols desore,
> Et d'autel fu sa robe tote (v. 3089-91)
> *vols* means 'turned, trimmed, edged.'

> N'an fist que trois et si morra
> Que ja mes forgier ne porra
> Espee nule apres cesti (v. 3155-57).

I read *morra* as 'will desist,' the future of *morer*, mod. French *demeurer*. The P MS has *jurra* for *morra*.

et terre tenist Et si granz bien an avenist" (v. 3587-90). He (Perceval) is in a state of mortal sin, she says, because his mother has died as a result of his having left her. She declares that the sword which he carries will fail him. He asks where it can be mended in such a case and she replies "au lac qui est sor Cotoatre" and that he must entrust it there to the smith who made it; his name is Trebuchet. Perceval begs her to leave the dead and come with him, the living. She refuses to abandon the body until it has been buried. Perceval sets out again. He meets a lady, in very sorry condition now, from whom he had taken a ring and many kisses in the course of his early adventures. He defeats her knight, li Orgueilleus de la Lande, who has been oppressing her because of that first meeting. It was li Orgueilleus who beheaded the slain knight outside the Grail Castle. There follows an extraneous episode in the course of which Perceval once more visits Arthur's court. A hideous damsel appears and denounces Perceval for his Grail failure while announcing other possible adventures which attract Gawain, etc. But Perceval wanders again, this time for five years without any memory of God. His sin has prevailed. On a Good Friday he is induced to visit a hermit and confess. At this point the Grail episode resumes once more. The hermit tells Perceval that in a chamber beyond the one where the Fisher King received his guest was a being who was fed by the Grail bread or *oiste* alone. This being has not left the chamber for a long time (specified differently in the manuscripts, some as fifteen, others as twelve years, and so on). This being is the brother of the hermit and of Perceval's mother. He is the father of the Fisher King. The hermit absolves Perceval from the guilt of his mother's death.

> Einsi Percevaus reconut
> Que Deus au vandredi reçut
> Mort et si fu crocefiiez (v. 6509-11).

Our predecessors have spent much time sketching in a "romantic" background of sources which could have been drawn upon by a creative imagination such as they attribute to Chrétien de Troyes. Their interpretation draws no pattern of meaning from the literal level. In mediaeval technique the poet began with a fairly coherent story (the *matière*) through which he thought to achieve an expression of *sens* on various other levels: the allegorical, moral and anagogical.[4] In order to prove a consistent pattern in the *sens* the salient details in the *matière* must be consistently accounted for.

The reasoning of those who have discussed the Grail has begun too often with *a priori* conceptions upon which they have later sought to make scattered comparisons which might fit. With the exception of the ritualist cult solutions, which were advanced by Jessie L. Weston, and at one time by W. A. Nitze, the investigators have not begun with a clean slate—listing important details and proceeding from these to a solution. The Christian ritual theory was forced upon us by the next generation after Chrétien which chose the only explanation that could have seemed logical in their day. The Celtic theory for the Grail thrust itself upon us because many of us believe that the motifs of Chrétien's earlier works are undeniably Celtic. That he might have had a change of theme, with his change of patron, when he left the service of Henri de Champagne for Philippe d'Alsace, is not taken strongly into consideration. The nature cults that have been proposed do offer a freer opportunity for independent judgment, but unfortunately we know almost nothing about the Eleusinian Mysteries and Adonis cult. We have little guarantee

---

[4] The relation of *sens* and *matière* was studied very brilliantly by Nitze in Romania XLIV (1915), 14-36. Nitze speaks of "une bele conjointure ou 'combinaison,' développée suivant le *sans* de l'auteur" which gives it value in the eyes of the public for whom Chrétien wrote (p. 17). I cannot believe that a hodgepodge of Celtic and Byzantine Christian material can be called "une bele conjointure." Of course Nitze thought of the Grail romance as an instruction book for "la jeunesse" (p. 35). We have added above a little of the doctrine of the three levels of symbolic interpretation to Nitze's statement. This method of reading with three types of spiritual meaning "was used in practice by the author of the Epistle to the Hebrews, and to less extent by others of his time. The first clear statement of the method, however, is that of John Cassian: . . . the letter told of past events, while in allegory was to be found instruction as to belief, in trope as to duty, and in anagoge as to the eternal goal toward which led the faithful keeping of creed and commandments." (H. Flanders Dunbar, *Symbolism in Mediaeval Thought*, Yale Press, 1929, p. 498). In Chapter 11 of the Epistle to the Hebrews, which was certainly read by Chrétien, if (as we believe) he made use of Chapter 9, there is a beautiful symbolism of the Achievements of Faith as illustrated in the deeds of the Hebrew Patriarchs.

that these persisted with any strength during eight hundred years of Christianity in western Europe. The solution found in the Welsh *Peredur* is hardly worthy of consideration.

Details which do not seem to be fortuitous are among the following. There are two men in the boat—not one. The Fisher King is baiting his hook with *fish*, to catch fish. This is a more violent form of fishing which does not agree with what we should expected if the Fisher King were intended to be Christ. I believe that a net would have been the device described, in this case, by Chrétien. The Grail hall is peculiar. What are the *loges* which precede the hall itself? Why is that hall a perfect square? Surely the columns of *arain* or copper are not mentioned because that was a common material for such columns in France or England. The Fisher King himself must have been an individual of great distinction to give point to the Grail episode. If he were just an uncle of Perceval, with no unusual qualities the tale would fall flat as it does in the Welsh *Peredur*. Why are his garments edged with purple? The Grail when it appears is attended by light—hardly a condition surrounding a Celtic cauldron of plenty. It is undeniably a vessel that provides food, however, that satisfies hunger of a bodily kind. It can produce venison and other varieties of physical meats. I should not say that it was merely a source of food for the spirit. It is carried by a feminine figure, and this is indeed a hard enigma for those who prefer the Christian ritual explanation. What is the *taule* or *tailleor*, a sheet or plate of silver which is brought in with equal solemnity? There are just two maidens; the other members of the procession are men. From the lance blood drips upon the hand of the squire who carries it. I have a distinct feeling that no one who was a Christian would treat in this way the Blood of Our Lord. Remember that Joseph of Arimathea used a vessel to receive the Sacred Blood. Giotto in his mural at Assisi has angels collecting the Blood from the Cross. Such a picture of dripping blood as Chrétien gives reminds one more of a sacrifice of a carnal kind. Why was the Fisher King lame? There is no record in Christian authority that Christ was lame after the Resurrection. Who was there in Celtic tradition who fits this description? It is important to know just why a state of mortal sin would keep Perceval from resolving the Grail tragedy, for a tragedy it seems to have been. It is difficult to understand how Perceval could have made the great Dagda any happier by inquiring after his cauldron of plenty and the poisonous spear of Fiacail, or the Luin of Celtchar held vertically over a cauldron of blood. We are told that the solution of the Grail tragedy by Perceval would result in great good. In this the nature cult solution seems more logical, because we assume then that the healing of the Adonis or the ailing king would bring about at least a season of spring. By the Christian interpretation all that can result is an adoration of the Host by Perceval individually. The Celtic themes hold that the land would be thus saved from enchantment. We could multiply such questions as these, but the results will continue to be the same. If the Grail solution does not have greater meaning than has been suggested so far, then the words of the damsel who nurses the headless body of her knight are a meaningless exaggeration.

I believe that the Castle of the Grail was a symbolical representation of the Temple of Solomon in Jerusalem, colored with some of the trappings of mediaeval feudalism. The Grail, the lance, the blood, the silver plate were the vessel of manna, Aaron's rod (which took many forms in the tradition as we shall presently see), the blood of sacrifice made by the High Priest, and the tablet of the Law. These were sacred objects preserved in the Holy of Holies, a large square, or rather cubical, chamber, which the High Priest of the Temple visited once a year. "Into the second [Tabernacle] went the high priest alone once every year, not without blood, which he offered for himself, and for the errors of the people" (Epistle to the Hebrews, 9.7). In the Grail Castle the High Priest was that great father of the Tribes of Israel, Jacob, who was lame as a result of his struggle with the Angel of the Lord. Over the Ark in the Holy of Holies were two "Cherubim obumbrantia propitiatorium," or 'shadowing the mercy seat.' [5] Although these were images in actual fact, for his dramatic effect Chrétien was obliged to have the table of the Law and the vessel of manna borne in by human beings not too removed in popular imagination from Cherubim,

---

[5] ". . . and the ark of the covenant laid around with gold, wherein was the golden pot that had manna, and Aaron's rod that budded, and the tables of the covenant; And over it the cherubims of glory shadowing the mercyseat; of which we cannot now speak particularly" (Ep. Hebr. 9. 4-5).

and so these are carried in by maidens.[6] The Quest of the Holy Grail, in our opinion, was the conversion of the Jewish Temple to Christianity. That was the great good that would result, which would restore Jacob to his health and to his estates. In the words of St. Paul in the Epistle to the Hebrews, which I have already quoted from above, "the way into the holiest of all was not yet made manifest . . . as the first tabernacle was yet standing . . . which stood only in meats and drinks, and divers washings and carnal ordinances, imposed on them until the time of reformation" (9.8-10). Paul goes on to say that when the Blood of Christ entered into the holy place all this became unnecessary. The blood of the new testament will suffice for the redemption of the transgressions that were under the first testament.

In our belief it was St. Paul's Epistle to the Hebrews which was the inspiration for the Quest of the Grail. In a way it is attested by the text of Chrétien that he had been recently handling this Epistle. Chrétien quotes from the fourth chapter of the First Epistle of John which is only some one or two folios before the Epistle of Paul to the Hebrews,[7] if we can imagine Chrétien having in his hands a MS containing the Pauline and other Epistles of the New Testament. Such a MS would not have been so conveniently supplied with page heading and display titles as we have now come to expect. If Chrétien turned back to the first Epistle of John and thought he was still reading St. Paul it must have been because he had been perusing something of St. Paul's a few minutes previously. This is the passage in the Perceval to which we are referring:

> Deus est charitez, et qui vit
> Au charité, selonc l'escrit,

---

[6] The Talmudic tradition speaks of Cherubim as having child-like faces. In the Robert Estienne Latin Bible (Paris, 1546), which I have, there is a plate showing these Cherubim of the Ark, on folio 21. They are distinctly feminine in dress and in hair arrangement. "The Cherubim placed by God at the entrance of Paradise were angels created on the third day, and therefore they had no definite shape; appearing either as men or women, or as spirits or angelic beings." This is from the *Jewish Encyclopedia*, under CHERUB.

[7] Professor Kenneth W. Clark of Duke University, a specialist in New Testament, is our authority that the Epistles of John preceded rather than followed the Epistle to the Hebrews in the mediaeval manuscripts of the New Testament.

> Sainz Pos le dit et *je le lui*
> Il maint an Deu et Deu an lui   (v. 48-51).

Please note that Chrétien comments that he had read with his own eyes: *je le lui*.

The Epistle to the Hebrews was addressed to Christian Jews who were in danger of falling away from the gospel. It is basically a comparison between Judaism and Christianity stating that Judaism is "only the earthly shadow of the heavenly realities that Jesus Christ came to establish and bring within our reach." [8] The priesthood of Christ is contrasted with the Levitical priesthood. The heart of the Epistle is in Chapter 9 which, we contend, contains the core of Chrétien's Grail procession. The validity of the New Testament (playing upon the two meanings of the word) is derived from His death. The sacrifice in the Old Testament must be repeated yearly; Christ's sacrifice was for once and all. Christ entered the tabernacle in His own blood after the Crucifixion. This we contend is the doctrine which Chrétien was presenting in the form of his Romance.

In support of our theory that the Grail Castle is a mediaeval dramatization of the issues in Hebrews chapter 9 we will pass in review most of the details contained in the Grail episode and see how they can be explained in terms of the Old Testament and of Jewish oral tradition, notably by the Midrashim. Of inestimable help in this connection are the six volumes compiled by Louis Ginzberg with index in the seventh volume by Booz Cohen, entitled (in English translation) *The Legends of the Jews* and published in English by the Jewish Publication Society of America (1913-1938).

We will take the details in the order in which they occur in Chrétien's story. First there are the Fisher King and his companion in the boat. Ginzberg narrates for us the Midrash tradition about Jacob and his son Zebulon. This son of Jacob is, in my suggestion, the other man who was with the Fisher King in the boat. When Zebulon was one hundred and fourteen years of age, which was two years after the death of Joseph, he summoned his sons and counselled them: "When I was in Canaan, catching fish at the shores of the sea for my father Jacob, many were drowned in the waters of the sea, but I came away un-

---

[8] J. R. Dummelow, *The One Volume Bible Commentary* (New York, 1941), p. 1013.

harmed. For ye must know that I was the first to build a boat for rowing upon the sea, and I plied along the coasts in it, and caught fish for my father's household, until we went down into Egypt. Out of pity I would share my haul with the poor stranger, and if he was sick or well on in years, I would prepare a savory dish for him, and I gave unto each according to his needs, sympathizing with him in his distress and having pity upon him. Therefore the Lord brought numerous fish to my nets, for he that gives aught to his neighbor, receives it back from the Lord with great increase. For five years I fished in the summer, and in the winter I pastured the flocks with my brethren" (Ginzberg II, 205-6).

Again making use of the Midrashim, as interpreted by Ginzberg (II, 138), Jacob bestowed this blessing on his grandchildren: "May your names be named on Israel, and like unto fishes may you grow into a multitude in the midst of the earth, and as fishes are protected by the water, so may you be protected by the merits of Joseph." It is meant by this that the children of Joseph (the Ephraimites), who were descendants of Jacob, were likened to a multitude of fish. We have looked further for the motif which is represented by Jacob's baiting his hook, with fish as bait. He was sending little fish to be swallowed by bigger ones. This may be reminiscent of the Haggadah tradition in which the Ten Commandments are equated each with the ten words with which God created the world. To quote Ginzberg: "The Sixth Commandment: 'Thou shalt not kill,' corresponds to the word: 'Let the waters bring forth abundantly the moving creature,' for God said: 'Be not like the fish, among whom the great swallow the small'" (III, 105). For one acquainted with the Haggadah tradition the large fish being caught by means of the small suggests a breaking of the commandment which forbids violence. It is this association of Judaism with killing which is further illustrated in the Grail Castle.

The details of the Grail hall are reminiscent of what we know about the Temple of Solomon. The *loges* through which Perceval enters before he finds himself in the hall are porticoes before the front of the Temple: "porticum vero ante frontem" (2 Paralip. or Chronicles 3.4). Other correspondences are: the copper or brass pillars (3 Kings 7. 15-16); the square-shaped hall (2 Paralip. 3.8); Chrétien's table of ivory set upon trestles of *ebenus* which corresponds to the shewbread table with trestles of setim wood (Exodus 25.28). Concerning the Temple one Bible text says: "And he made ten candlesticks of gold according to their form and set them in the Temple, five on the right hand and five on the left." (2 Paralip. 4.7). These *candelabra aurea decem* surely did not mean ten-branched candelabra in the Temple of Solomon, but a mediaeval reader might be pardoned for interpreting in that way. The golden *urna* or Grail of the Second Tabernacle was filled with the manna of the Lord, the spiritual food of the Old Testament, and the inference would be that this manna fed the table of the Fisher King who, we suppose, is Israel or Jacob, the spiritual father of the Jews. Christ likened Himself to Jacob in John 1.49, while speaking to Nathaniel. "And he said unto him, Verily, verily, I say unto you, Hereafter ye shall see heaven open, and the angels of God ascending and descending upon the Son of man." The light around the Grail does not require much explanation when we know that sacred things were generally assumed to be accompanied by light. It is true, however, that the Tabernacle of the Lord when first erected was surrounded by "the appearance of fire by night" (Numbers 9.16).

Jacob was the father of the Levites or priests. He wore the high priest clothing which was first worn by Adam, the first born man in the world (Ginzberg I, 332; II, 139; V, 284). In this capacity it is perfectly correct for him to be in Chrétien's mind a symbol of the high priesthood, within the Holy of Holies of the Grail Castle. The sable garments which he wears are, to be sure, not those of the high priest; in this case they may denote mourning—sackcloth and ashes. But what of the purple edging? The Law of Moses (Numbers 15.38) required purple fringes upon the garments: "Loquere filiis Israel, et dices ad eos ut faciant sibi fimbrias per angulos palliorum, ponentes in eis vittas hyacinthinas . . ."

With regard to the meal that was served at the Grail feast we can explain the venison haunch which was placed before the King and Perceval. In Genesis 25.28 we learn that Isaac, the father, loved Esau "because he did eat of his venison." The Jewish oral law gives much more detail on this fondness of Isaac for venison. We will quote from Ginzberg (I, 331-7). Rebekah tells Jacob to prepare savory meat for his father that "he may bless thee before his death." She dressed Jacob in the garments of Esau, "the high-priestly raiment in which God had clothed

Adam, 'the first-born of the world,' " which had been descended from Adam through Noah, Shem, Abraham, and Isaac, to Esau. Jacob prepares the feast and says to his father, "Arise, I pray thee, sit and eat of my venison" (Ginzberg I, 336). Later when Esau appears Isaac tells him that Jacob's venison had marvellous qualities. Isaac said: "I had only to wish for bread, or fish, or locusts, or flesh of animals ... it had the taste of any dainty one could wish for."

On the manna which we assume was in the vessel of the Graal the Bible itself is very explicit. This fell and fed the Israelites during their forty years in the wilderness; only when they reached Gilgal and began to partake of grain did the manna cease. Aaron was instructed to gather some in a vessel and lay it before the testimony (Ex. 16.17-35; Josh. 5.10-12). The word *manna* meant "What is it"? (Ex. 16.15), a phrase used by the Israelites when they first saw it. The Rabbinical tradition (Ginzberg III, 44-45) states that the manna had different taste according to the wishes of those who partook of it. When some of it melted it was consumed by beasts in the field and their own flesh was impregnated with the taste. That is the only way that the unfaithful could taste of this spiritual food.

If Perceval were one of the unfaithful it was only through such flesh as venison that he could partake of the manna. Remember that each portion of venison, in Chrétien's story, was placed upon a whole *gastel* and served in that way. What were these *gastels*? I suggest that the *panes propositionis* or shew-bread are intended. These were loaves of unleavened bread, changed every Sabbath, which were placed upon the table of setim or shittim wood (Lev. 24.5-6).

If the Grail is not to be taken in this way—as the vessel of manna preserved in the Holy of Holies—if the Christian ritual theory is correct, how then can Perceval partake of it, in sin as he is, and after being fed by the Host how does he remain in this sin?

Critics of this theory may be puzzled by our equating of the bleeding lance with Aaron's budding rod. The Rabbinical tradition has it that God created this rod on the Sixth day of Creation (*Jewish Encyc.*). He gave it to Adam when the latter was driven from Paradise. From Adam it passed through the hands of Shem, Enoch, Abraham, Isaac, and Jacob. Jacob bestowed it upon Joseph. An Egyptian noble Jethro stole it and planted it in his garden whence it was rescued by Moses who married Jethro's daughter. The manner in which Moses obtained it is of special interest to us. The rod could not be pulled from the ground save by Moses who knew the name of God engraved upon it and uttered this. This motif is similar to that of the sword that cannot be pulled forth except by one hero for whom it is intended. According to the Haggadic modification of this tradition, King Josiah later concealed the rod and the Ark, and their whereabouts would remain unknown until the coming of the Messiah. There is still another legend (Ginzberg VI, 106-107) which identifies the rod of Aaron with the staff of the kings (Judah, David, and the Messiah). According to still another interpretation the rod is symbolic of the Temple to be built by the Messiah (*ibid.*). It was because Aaron's rod alone budded that he and his descendants were designated for the priesthood (Numbers 17.1-8).

The rod, of course, was capable of changing shape of its own accord when thrown upon the ground. It was the holy staff of Israel which early Christians desired in some way to associate with their own traditions. On the Day of Atonement when the High Priest visited the Altar of incense in the Tabernacle he tipped the horns or corners of this altar with sacrificial blood (Ex. 30.10). In the Epistle to the Hebrews we learn that "Moreover he sprinkled with blood both the tabernacle and *all the vessels of the ministry.*" A lance was the common variety of rod in use in the Middle Ages. Banners were fastened to it; it was a badge of authority, as was the rod among ancient peoples. I find no difficulty in seeing in the lance from which blood dropped upon the bearer's hand (there is no steady stream of blood suggested in the text) a symbol of the "rod of the Old Testament" with its mark of carnal sacrifice. It is entirely probable that the lance form (for the rod) was used in order to enable Chrétien to continue his allegory further when, at the dissolution of the Grail Castle, the Jewish relics should pass into the most sacred relics of the Passion. Just as Perceval knew his name (*Perce-voile?*) in advance of his achieving his quest to "penetrate the veil" (Leviticus 21.23), even so the lance of the Passion was thus prefigured in the rod of Aaron with its carnal blood of ritual sacrifice. The rod or lance of the Jews, after the accomplishment of the Quest, becomes the Sacred Lance which was stained only with Christ's Blood. This transformation is not figured in exactly the same way but it is suggested by Origen (*In Exodus,* c. 7): "This rod of Moses by which Egypt was subdued is in a figure the Cross of Christ by which the world is conquered."

In a later passage, in the midst of Gawain adventures, the *vavassor* of Guinganbresil advises that Gawain be given a chance to go look for the bleeding lance (v. 6110-17) and he adds:

> E s'est escrit qu'il iert une ore
> Que toz li reaumes de Logres
> Qui ja dis fu la terre as ogres
> Sera destruiz par cele lance (v. 6168-71).

We take it that this refers to prophecies of destruction of England (Logres) by the Jews (which Chrétien must have known to be ridiculous). We know from Perceval's conversation with the damsel who held the beheaded knight in her arms that the essence of the Grail question, which would have brought about such good, was "Why is there blood on the lance?" (v. 3552-3):

> "Et demandastes vos por quoi
> Ele seignoit?"

The hideous damsel also chides him:

> Que tu ne poïs demander
> Por qoi cele gote de sanc
> Saut par la pointe del fer blanc (v. 4656-8).

The lance and its blood are the central motif of the theme. If we interpret correctly, this meant the carnal sacrifice of the Jews as opposed to the Sacrifice of the Body and Blood of Our Lord. It should not be forgotten that there was a dreadful massacre of the Jews at Blois in 1171, and Blois was associated with Troyes (Marie de Champagne's sister had married Thibaut de Blois), where the Jews were accused of using Christian blood in their sacrifice.[9]

---

[9] Feeling against the Jews began to run very high in England during 1187-88, although they were protected by Henry II for money reasons. On the day of Richard's Coronation (Sept. 3, 1189) a notable massacre was inflicted upon the Jews of Lincoln. See Joseph Jacobs, *The Jews of Angevin England* (London, 1893). Walter Map in a humorous statement, made apropos of his duties as an itinerant justice, remarked that he would give justice to all but Cistercians and Jews (Giraldus Cambrensis, *Speculum Ecclesiae* LV, 219-20). The Christians in England were irritated by the increase in wealth and power of the Jewish people in their midst.

The quest of the lance by Gawain is contrasted with the quest by Perceval, in Chrétien's mind. Gawain will seek to overthrow the lance by violent means. Perceval's quest will be accomplished by persuasion, by asking the Grail question. The motif of the Question which opens the way is a favorite in Jewish tradition. My friend A. H. Schutz informs me that in the Haggadah tradition the Passover ceremony begins with four questions that must be asked by the youngest person (the greatest fool?). The most important is: "Why is this night different from all others?" We are not forcing a comparison between the Passover and the Grail; but the question motif is there.

The gift of the sword which shall fail in only one special condition also offers itself for a solution along similar lines. The *sore pucelle* we will not identify for the moment. She is a descendant (*nièce*) of the King. The smith who made the sword manufactured only three. In the Epistle to Hebrews (chapter 4) St. Paul says: "For the word of God is quick and powerful, and sharper than any two edged sword. . . ." Abelard in his famous Commentary *In Epistolam ad Hebraeos* gave the accepted explanation for the word of God as a sword: "Et hoc est, quia 'sermo,' id est Filius Dei, Christus videlicet." [10] If Christ is as a sword there are two others like it, the Father and the Holy Ghost. Christ (the word of God) was sent to Perceval as a sword that would fail him in only one case. Need we ask what this case would be? There sat Perceval wrapped in the red mantle (of mortal sin), the one case (in the Doctrine of Penance) when Christ cannot avail. If Perceval had not been in mortal sin he could have asked the Grail question and with Christ's help could have freed the King from the Old Testament Covenant, and that meant all the Jews, from the Old Law. Scarlet, as Isaiah said, was the color of sin: "Though your sins be as scarlet . . ." (1.18). This is the one proper designation for a cloak of mortal sin. See also Apocalypse 17.3-4.

Who was the girl with the beheaded knight in her arms? The obvious answer is that this knight was representative of John the Baptist, who lost his head in an endeavor to accomplish a similar quest. I said that I might identify the *sore pucelle*, the

---

[10] Arthur Landgraf, *Commentarius Cantabrigiensis in Epistolas Pauli e schola Petri Abaelardi in Epistolam ad Hebraeos* (Notre Dame, 1945), p. 719.

nièce of Jacob, who sent the sword (the Word of God, Christ). Presumably this is Mary, the Virgin. Beauty of a feminine kind was usually designated in the Twelfth century by reference to blond locks.

What is the lake beside Cotoatre? The name *Cotoatre* suggests a Gallicization of such a name as *Kotoath*, although I have not found such a name.[11] The smith who made the sword, and who alone can mend it is called Trebuchet. One of the meanings of this word is that of 'assaying scales.' Such scales would symbolize the Justice of God. God is Justice (Deut. 32.4). He made the sword. If we are correct in assuming that Perceval will find that it fails him while he is in sin, then Penance alone will repair it. (Perceval subsequently fights with this sword against li Orgueilleus and it does not fail, although the damsel had told him it would be of no use to him. But then li Orgueilleus was a special case. Sagramors and Kay later are unhorsed by lance alone.) [12]

In our resumé above we did not list the motifs which preceded the episode of the Grail Castle. We should like to mention them, giving details as we go. These fit well into our framework. Perceval's mother informed him about Christianity when she explained the Church to him:

>"Une maison bele et saintisme
>Et de cors sainz et de tresors.
>S'i sacrefie l'an le cors
>Jesucrist, la prophete sainte,
>Cui Giu firent honte mainte; (v. 578-82)
>. . . . .
>Vos lo gie au mostier aler."
>"Donc irai je mout volantiers

---

[11] I now suggest Kattath in Joshua 19.15 as the base of this Cotoatre. Kattath is one of the cities allotted to the children of Zebulon. The lake which is nearby is the Sea of Galilee.

[12] Kay, of course, is an Arthurian character of long standing, but his role in the symbolism of the Grail is that of Pride. Sagramors, who is also overthrown by Perceval, can be translated literally as 'Sycamore tree.' The famous legendary tree of that species was in Egypt. Aetheria claimed in the *Peregrinatio* to have seen it: "Et est ibi praeterea arbor sicomori, quae dicitur a patriarchis posita esse. . . . Hoc autem referente sancto episcopo de Arabia cognovimus; nam ipse nobis dixit nomen ipsius arboris, quemadmodum apellant eam graece, id est dendros alethiae, quod nos dicimus arbor veritatis" (8,3).

As iglises et as mostiers,"
Fet li vaslez, 'd'ore an avant
Einsi le vos met an covant.' (v. 594-98)

This is the first real introduction of Perceval to Christianity. He has no baptized name as yet; he is merely *biaus fils*. His father

Fu parmi les janbes navrez
Si que il maheigna del cors.
Sa granz terre, ses granz tresors
Que il avoit come prodon,
Ala tot a perdicion. (v. 436-40)

This father bears strong resemblance to the Fisher King, whom we have so far identified as Jacob, the symbol of Israel. The damsel in the tent, which Perceval mistakes for a church, from whom he takes the emerald ring (emerald represents the stone of the Levites placed in the Holy Ark) is strongly rebuked by her knight, li Orgueilleus de la Lande (Herod?), who accuses her wrongly of lack of chastity with the young Perceval and who says that henceforth she shall be oppressed by him until Perceval is beheaded. We suggest that the damsel is representative of Judaea. It will be recalled by our *résumé* above that Perceval eventually overcomes li Orgueilleus de la Lande and causes the oppression of the lady to be lifted.

To return to the earlier episodes. After leaving this lady in the tent Perceval stops for a brief time in Arthur's court (long enough to have a brush with Kay) and then follows a knight in red who has snatched Arthur's golden cup. He wants the knight's armor. This knight, if we follow out our allegory, must be "worldliness" or something similar. After killing the red knight Perceval takes his arms but refuses to give up entirely the simple garments furnished him by his good mother. This refusal to abandon his simple clothing is emphasized over and over, so that we can be certain it had some meaning for Chrétien. Gornemanz, the *prod'home*, whom he then visits, finally persuades Perceval to leave off completely his mother's clothing and her instructions. We identify this Gornemanz with *Li Sages*, or Ecclesiastes. Gornemanz is continually quoting from Ecclesiastes in his instruction:

> Et li Sages dit et retret;
> Qui trop parole, pechié fet.
> Por ce, biaus frere, vos chasti
> De trop parler . . . (v. 1653-56)

The general trend of remarks in Ecclesiastes is to reform the "fool."

At this point something must be said about the events that take place in Arthur's Court before the hero sets forth to stop the Red Knight. He is mocked by Kay. His future greatness, however, is proclaimed by the lowest man present—a jester—and by a maid. Kay slaps the girl for this and Perceval vows to avenge the blow, upon Kay. Obviously the characters of Arthur's Court are not to be treated as *personnes à clef*. They were already fixed as types in Chrétien's mind, and in those of most of his hearers. But the motifs of these scenes are strongly reminiscent of passages in the Wisdom books of the Bible. We suggest that Chrétien was here using the Arthurian characters to set the theme of his Grail quest. The Ecclesiastes says: "Better is a poor and wise child than an old and foolish king, who will no more be admonished" (4.13). "Wisdom is better than strength; nevertheless the poor man's wisdom is despised, and his words are not heard" (9.16). In the Song of Solomon the girl who calls out to her beloved says: "I called him . . . The watchmen . . . thy smote me" (5.7). The character of Kay is more or less a personification of Pride and Vanity wherever it is met with. Perceval's desire to humble Kay, although a natural one, suggests: "When pride cometh, then cometh shame" (Proverbs 11.1) and also "Pride goeth before destruction and an haughty spirit before a fall" (*ibid.*, 16.18).

Perceval meets with still another influence before he has the adventure of the Grail Castle. He comes to the castle of Blancheflor. She admits that she is a relative of Gornemanz. She is a lovely blond lady dressed in regal purple with vair and sable fur. She is in great distress at the time as she is sore pressed by King Clamadeus and his seneschal Anguingueron. She is chaste, for she lies in bed with Perceval and makes no attack on his virtue. Also she will not send him out of her own volition against the knight of superior force, Anguingueron or (as I would interpret it) Angigneron. For her Perceval overcomes Angigneron, and finally Clamadeus (after a brief siege). The defeat of the latter is made possible because God sends providentially ships with provisions for the castle. (We learn at a later stage, from the lips of the hermit who confesses Perceval that the prayers of Perceval's mother brought this about and thus saved Perceval from imprisonment.) She admits her relation to Gornemanz, who for us is *Li Sages*, but her environment is profoundly Christian. There are two religious houses in the town.[13] The people of Belrepaire commend the hero knight to the Holy Cross as he goes out to fight Anguingueron or Angigneron. The lady remarks that so many good men have died for her; that it is only right she should be discomforted. I have no trouble in identifying this Blancheflor de Belrepaire with

---

[13] The Castle of Belrepaire, or 'Fair Retreat,' is dominated by "Christian Thought." While it is besieged by Anguingueron and Clamadeus, Perceval

> Trova anhermies les rues
> Et les meisons viez decheues;
> Qu'ome ne fame n'i avoit.
> *Deus mostiers* an la vile avoit,
> Qui estoient deus abaies:
> Li une de nonains esbaies,
> Li autres de moines esgarez.
> Ne trova mie bien parez
> Les mostiers ne bien portanduz . . . (1753-61)

When Perceval goes out to fight Anguingueron:

> Biaus sire, *icele voire croiz*
> Ou Deus sofri pener son fil,
> Vos gart hui de mortel peril (2154-6)

is the cry which is raised by the people of Belrepaire "a une voix." When Blancheflor comes to Perceval's bed at night, weeping, she admonishes him:

> "Ha! jantis chevaliers, merci!
> Por Deu vos pri et *por son fil*
> Que vos ne m'an aiiez plus vil
> De ce que je sui ci venue."

She says of herself:

> "Par moi sont tant prodome mort,
> S'est droiz que je m'an desconfort" (1011-2).

This must refer to the martyrs of the Faith. Later (4204-10) when Perceval sees the blood upon the snow he thinks of Blancheflor.

Wisdom, Christian Wisdom, as descended from, but opposed to, the Jewish Wisdom of Gornemanz. Although Perceval overcomes for her Angigneron 'deceiver' (*Engignerie* is Old French for 'deceit' or 'trickery') and, with some help from Providence, Clamadeus, who is stronger but whose name certainly means 'accuser of God,' still the knight is not yet a Christian. He prays that God may place his mother, if she is dead, into the Bosom of Abraham:

> Que Deus el sain saint Abraham
> Le mete avuec les pies ames   (v. 2966-7)

and he commends the people of Belrepaire to the king of kings, which has Old Testament flavor.[14] Perceval (as we must continue to call him even before he knows his name) wants very much to return to Belrepaire and promises to do so. He does not have a name until after he leaves the Grail Castle when he unconsciously and vaguely admits that he is Perceval:

> Et cil qui son non ne savoit
> Devine et dit que il avoit
> Percevaus li Galois a non,
> N'il ne set s'il dit voir ou non;
> Mes *il dist voir*, et *si nel sot* (v. 3573-77).

It is evident that Chrétien attached special significance to the name. Perceval "divines" his name because of the *sens* which it implies. Perceval suggests *perce voile*, one who is destined to pierce the veil which shuts off the innermost Holy of Holies. It is then after he knows his name, that our protagonist mentions the Savior for the first time (v. 3496) since leaving his mother (v. 172-3).

Belrepaire, the stronghold of Blancheflor, is surrounded by Waste Land. This might be expected when a castle has been besieged for a length of time; but we are reminded here of the words of the Wisdom of Solomon: "*Wisdom* delivered the righteous men who fled from the fire ... Of whose wickedness even to this day the *waste land* that showeth is an testimony" (10.6-7).

---

[14] It is true that the "bosom of Abraham" and "King of Kings" were phrases not uncommon among Christians. But if Chrétien deliberately did not wish his hero to mention the name of Christ, they were useful expressions.

Next comes our most important problem. Who is the being who is within the inner chamber to which the vessel of manna is carried? This manna is a spiritual food which, according to the Jewish tradition is the food of the angels. "Man did eat angel's food; He sent them meat to the full" (Psalm 78.25) : This refers to manna. Furthermore when Christ was in the wilderness "angels ministered unto him." These two concepts placed side by side could mean that Christ while fasting in the earthly sense was fed by angels with spiritual food. I mean that such an idea could have been held in the Middle Ages. The room of the Fisher King was the Holiest of Holies of the first covenant, of the Jewish Temple. "But Christ being come an high priest of good things to come, by a greater and more perfect tabernacle, not made with hands, that is to say, not of this building (Epist. Hebr. 9.11). . . . For Christ is not entered into the holy places made with hands, which are the figures of the true; but into heaven itself . . . nor yet that he should offer himself often, as the high priest entereth into the holy place every year with the blood of others" (*ibid.*, 9.24-25).

In other words, Christ in the new covenant does not make use of the Jewish Holy of Holies but of a far finer tabernacle—which is Heaven in symbol. And Christ is not a high priest after the order of Aaron but after the order of the new covenant (Melchisedec). "If, therefore, perfection were by the Levitical priesthood . . . what further need was there that another priest should rise after the order of Melchisedec and not be called after the order of Aaron? For the priesthood being changed there is made of necessity a change also of the law (Epist. Hebr. 7.11-12). For it is evident that Our Lord sprang out of Judah of which tribe Moses spake nothing concerning priesthood. And it is yet far more evident: for that after the similitude of Melchisedec there arises another priest, Who is made, not after the law of a carnal commandment, but after the power of an endless life (*ibid.*, 7.14-15) . . . For there is verily a disannulling of the commandments going before, the weakness and unprofitableness thereof" (*ibid.*, 7.18).

According to the Christian ritual interpretation of the Grail Quest, the being in this inner room, whoever he is, is served by the Sacred Host, the Corpus Domini, and that alone. (This makes it impossible to identify him with the Holy Ghost.) The *oiste* in the Grail could hardly be a consecrated Host. We identify it with the spiritual food borne by the damsel who personifies one of the Cherubim ministering unto Christ. This manna

> il est si espiritaus
> Qu'a sa vie plus ne convient
> Que l'oiste qui el graal vient. (6426-28)

We assume, therefore, that Christ the high priest of the new Covenant is symbolically present in the room beyond the Jewish Holy of Holies. It is a vague place, not described. Perceval is not aware of it although he sees the Grail disappear in that direction. It is out of this world. One difficulty seems to remain. It is stated that the inner being has not left that chamber:

> Quinze anz a ja esté einsi
> Que fors de la chambre n'issi
> ou le graal veis antrer. (6429-31)

The symbolical meaning of the number fifteen may escape us. On the other hand it is possible to interpret it by the Kabbalah. The fifteenth letter of the Hebrew alphabet is Samech which has the value of sixty. If the "quinze anz" is not to be taken literally, and I do not see how any of the Grail story could have been set in exact time, then the *sens* of that number can best be explained by Numerology, the process of *gematria* in the Kabbalah. Sixty, of course, is an indefinite round number (Ginzberg I, 120, 303).[15] Chaucer refers to "sixty bokes olde and newe" that he possessed (*Leg. Good Women* G, 273) which is assumed to be a round, indefinite number. The number of years that had elapsed between the Ascension and the era of Arthur and his knights could not even be guessed at by an intelligent man of the Twelfth century. The copyists of the *Conte del Graal* were not sure of the "quinze anz." Some substituted *douze*, others *vint* in this particular passage.

The hermit says that he and the mother of Perceval are "brother and sister" of the King in the inner chamber. Being

---

[15] "Sixty. The large unit of the sexagesimal system used to express an indefinitely larger number," quoted from the article NUMBERS in the *Jewish Encyclopedia*. "... the later gematria ... by which the numerical equivalents of letters and words were made a means of interpretation." See Hastings, *Encyclopedia of Religion and Ethics*, under KABBALAH. Important examples of the use of sixty as an indefinitely large number are in the Song of Songs 3.7 and 6.8.

Christians they are of one blood with Christ. But the Fisher King is only a child of God, being a Jew. The Grail question, we assume, would have opened up the inner chamber to Jacob and the Jews would have been freed from their sorrows and tribulations. Many lives would be saved, thereby. As it was, Jacob like Perceval partook of the manna only in the form of the venison placed upon the *gastels*, while in the Holy of Holies.

I believe that Philippe d'Alsace, the new protector of Chrétien, whom Chrétien praises enthusiastically for his charity and generosity, gave to Chrétien the task of developing in a popular or romance form the theme of the conversion of the Jewish people to Christianity. Chrétien says:

> Ce est li contes del Graal
> Don li cuens li baille le livre. (v. 66-7)

This book may have been a MS of the Epistles of St. Paul, with, in particular, the Epistle addressed to the Hebrews.[16] We know today St. Paul was not actually the author of the Epistle to the Hebrews, but he was thought to be so in Chrétien's time.

If Chrétien were assigned this task of elaborating on the theme of conversion from Judaism to Christianity it is not unlikely that there was a basic reason for his selection. Our assumption is that he himself was a Perceval—a converted Jew who was given the *Crestianus* at the time of his baptism. It has been established beyond much reasonable doubt that *Crestiens li Gois* who signed the *Philomena* was a Jew, and from his name, he was certainly a Christianized one.[17] Raphael Levy will not agree that this

---

[16] And yet Chrétien in his description of the hideous damsel (v. 4616-19) says:

> Et se les paroles sont voires
> Teus con li livres les devise,
> Onques riens si leide a devise
> Ne fu neis dedanz anfer.

This passage would indicate that Chrétien's source book was a rather detailed account of his plot. Furthermore in v. 2806-7 the *estoire* is again mentioned—as authority for the dress of Kay! In v. 3261-2, the same *estoire* states that the table top in the Grail hall was all of one piece! This citing of the authority for minor details of description is a device of a conventional kind.

[17] "Ce conte Crestiens li Gois" (*Philomena*, v. 734-8, ed. C. deBoer).

Crestiens li Gois was our Chrétien.[18] On this I disagree strongly. I am in accord with those who think that *Crestiens li Gois* and Chrétien de Troyes were one and the same. To be sure, we are not obliged to assume that our poet was a Jew in order to explain his knowledge of Jewish oral tradition. After all, we know that he was a resident of the town of Troyes in Champagne, and that Troyes had been the seat of rabbinical schools of international importance since the time of Rashi (d. 1105).

For me an *argumentum ex silentio* is that Chrétien never signed as witness any of the many cartularies which were executed for the Count of Champagne. We know that such documents were witnessed by those who happened to be present in the *salle* when they were drawn up, depending upon the social position of those present.[19] Apparently Chrétien did not have much social position. If he were a converted Jew this would have been the case. Of course, he could have been a common Christian *jongleur*. But such an assumption hardly fits the dignity and learning which the poet of the *Yvain*, *Lancelot*, etc., displays.

Be it understood that I am not attacking the theory of Celtic origins for the motifs in Chrétien's earlier works. Rather I am even offering a better explanation of how he could have come upon much of this same material. As Troyes was a center of Jewish learning, students came there from Lincoln and other points in Great Britain. Nor am I attacking the obvious fact that Robert of Boron and the Continuators of Chrétien thought of the whole Grail story as a purely Christian one. The only contention which we wish to make is that in the mind of Chrétien, and in that of Philippe d'Alsace, the Grail story was the conversion of Judaism to Christianity. This original purpose was not clear to later writers on the Grail theme, which includes the compiler of the Welsh *Peredur*. (Incidentally this would make it quite evident that the *Peredur* followed Chrétien's *Perceval* in date of composition.)

This interpretation that we seek to give to the Grail serves Chrétien better than other theories have done. It shows him to have been an artist who could be represented in pale tones beside the greater and far more magnificent figure of Dante. After all,

---

[18] *PMLA*, XLVI (1931), 312-20.
[19] "Social Status at the Court of King John," *Speculum*, XII (1937), 319-29.

Chrétien would deserve an almost unique place for his romantic representation of a problem and a solution which was a burning one to his contemporaries. And, as one of my kind critics has recently said, there is grandeur in the thought that Chrétien, if he were a converted Jew, was telling on a greater scale his own life story and conversion in this Quest of the Grail. His Quest had an ending, while the Quest of Perceval had none.

EPILOGUE

In note 12 we refer somewhat vaguely to the symbolism of the sycamore tree, quoting from a tradition recorded in the *Peregrinatio* of the late fourth, or possibly the mid sixth, century. In the *Lancelot,* or *Chevalier de la Charrette* (vv. 7005-13) Chrétien de Troyes mentions an ancient sycamore under which the king sits as he witnesses the combat between Meleagant and Lancelot:

> An la lande un sagremor ot
> Si bel que plus estre ne pot:
> Mout tenoit place, mout iert lez,
> S'est li leus tot an tor orlez
> De menue erbe fresche et bele,
> Qui an toz tans estoit novele.
> Soz le sagremor jant et bel
> Qui plantez fu del tans Abel,
> Sort une clere fontenele . . .

It is a question whether this particular tree also symbolizes Truth.

On p. 19 we have identified *Angigneron* with the word for deceit. Dr. Engstrom has called to my attention a passage in Gustave Cohen's *Histoire de la mise en scène au moyen-âge* (Paris, 1906), p. 221: "Le diable *Enguignart* porte un surcot bleu à capuce rouge. Il a voulu se déguiser en jeune dandy du temps." Cohen takes this from MS 579 of Besançon (14th century) which contains a *mystère* entitled *Le jour du jugement*.

The hideous damsel who appears riding upon a yellow or tawny mule is more ugly than anything in Hell. She begins by upbraiding Perceval because he failed to take Fortune by the forelock and ask the questions concerning the three cardinal things in the Grail Castle: the Blood, the Grail, and the Being in the inner room. If he had taken the golden opportunity to ask these questions the Fisher King would have been cured and held his lands in peace, but now there will be many widows and orphans because of Perceval. Then she turns abruptly to the king and announces two quests: that of the Chastel Orgueilleus and that of the damsel on the hill below Montesclaire and the sword with the strange sword-knots. This last is the great quest, she says, and will bring praise, and happiness from God. (*Perceval*, vv. 4610-4717).

Be it noted that the other two individuals who chide Perceval for not asking the Grail questions, namely, the lady outside the castle (3591 ff.) and the Hermit whom he will visit later (6339 ff.) both understand that he could not ask the questions because of his sin, deriving from the death of his mother. Only the hideous damsel sneers because he failed to take a good chance when it came his way. Fortune's head is bald behind; Perceval will not be able to seize her again. The damsel then suggests other quests extraneous to the Grail. Perhaps it is a little farfetched to make comment upon her mule, in the light of Jewish law. In Leviticus 19.19 it is forbidden to breed mules; although many were used later by the Jews, particularly when brought from Babylon. In Leviticus 13.30,32,36, yellow hair is the sign of leprosy. There is apparent significance in the fact that in the very large index to Ginzberg (*op. cit.*) there is no entry under "yellow." Clearly the hideous damsel, who was uglier than anything in Hell, who had the eyes of a rat, the nose of a cat or monkey, the lips of an ox or ass, and teeth the color of the yolk of an egg, with the beard of a goat, and a hump on her breast and another on her back, is representative of some deadly Sin.[20] Perhaps she is Mortal Sin itself. It is after her visit that Perceval wanders for five years without thought of God (*Perceval,* vv. 6217 ff.).

Miss Helen Adolf has reminded me that later in the *Perceval* when Chrétien speaks of the Crucifixion he adds:

> Li fel giu par lor anvie,
> Qu'an devroit tuer come chiens,
> Firent lor mal et nos granz biens
> Quant il an la croiz le leverent . . . (vv. 6292-5).

Miss Adolf admits that this can be interpreted variously so that it does not really clarify our understanding of Chrétien's attitude toward the Jews. Perhaps the poet was contrasting "li fel" with "les bons." Christ was crucified by the "wicked Jews."

---

[20] Dr. Engstrom informs me that in the *'Oseh Fele,* II, 36a ff. there is a legend of a "woman with the animal face." Elijah gives her medicine and changes her monstrosity into beauty. This reference is not available to us. Ginzberg (*op. cit.* I, 423) records some monstrous creatures half monkey, which came from the wilderness across the sea, appearing to a descendant of Esau.

The role played by Jacob in our interpretation of the *Conte dou Graal* coincides repeatedly with traditional beliefs among the Jews, as expressed by Ginzberg in his monumental work. We will list some additional examples briefly:

Abraham and Jacob are the two great patriarchs. The younger Haggadah, which is nationalistic, gives Jacob first place (V, 207, 275).

Jacob foresaw the terrestrial and heavenly Temple (III, 447; VI, 152). He wished to reveal the Messianic Era to his sons (II, 140; V, 366). Jacob is the symbol of God's Justice (V, 318).

Jacob's lameness is stressed (VI, 254). Aaron's rod once belonged to him (V, 412; VI, 106, 107). For Jacob's sake Israel was redeemed from Egyptian bondage and will be redeemed by the Messiah (V, 275).

"When Israel suffers or commits a sin, it is Jacob who feels it more than the other patriarchs, and accordingly his joy will be the greatest when the future Redemption comes" (V, 275).

Ginzberg records the fact[21] that the flag of the Tribe of Zebulon (whom we identify with the boat companion of the Fisher King, on p. 15 *supra*) had a white background with the representation of a ship thereon. This symbolized the tradition that the Tribe was especially concerned with the art of navigation. In this connection our note 11 is of interest. Kattath is the first town mentioned as being within the "inheritance of the children of Zebulon." We were not conscious of this association at the time we connected Kattath with Cotoatre beside the lake.

Ginzberg observes that Zebulon was the tribe that devoted itself especially to commerce and was therefore a go-between for Israel and other nations. The blessing which Moses bestowed upon them was "Rejoice, Zebulon, in thy going out in commercial enterprises; at thy instance shall many nations pray upon the sacred mountain of the Temple and offer their sacrifices." This is to be explained in this way. Those who traded with Zebulon often went on a visit to Jerusalem and were sometimes converted through the impression they gained of that city. (*op. cit.*, III, 459-60.)

Apropos of our identification of Cotoatre, and of Trebuchet as

---

[21] *op. cit.*, III, 237.

the "scale of God's Justice" (p. 22), we are reminded of the figure in the Provençal *Boeci*:

> Bella's la domna e granz per cosedenz ...
> e sa ma dextra la domna u libre te;
> toz aquel libres era de fog ardenz:
> zo's la iusticia al rei omnipotent.
> si l'om forfai e pois no s'en repen,
> et evers Deu no'n faz' amendament,
> quora que's vol, ab aquel fog l'encent,
> ab aquel fog s'en pren so vengament.   (vv. 243, 246 ff.)

In brief, God's Justice is both a scale and a fire.

A discussion of the identity of Crestiens li Gois, in relation to that of Chrétien de Troyes, usually takes into account the relative frequency of the name itself. In the Parisian taille list of 1292 (*Paris sous Philippe-le-Bel, la Taille de Paris en 1292*, Paris, 1837) there are some 11,000 men listed. Only seven have the name *Crestien*. In the four taille lists of Paris, Karl Michaëlsson has counted 2020 occurrences of *Jehan* and 1181 of *Guillaume*. The twenty-fifth name, in order of descending frequency, is *Robin* with 90 instances. (See Karl Michaëlsson, *Etudes sur les noms de personne français d'après les Rôles de taille parisiens*, Uppsala, 1927, p. 60). The comparison is not exact as Michaëlsson is considering 13,000 men who appear from 1292 to 1313, counting each person, as far as he can ascertain, only once. Perhaps a percentage figure is better: his frequency for *Jehan* is 13.3 percent; *Guillaume* is 8.1. In my count, *Crestien* is about .00063. The name *Christiano monacho* is found once only in the mortuary roles of the twelfth century published by Léopold Delisle (*Rouleaux des morts*, Paris, 1866, p. 268). It is hardly correct, therefore, to begin a discussion with the assumption that *Crestien* was a common name.

Guernes de Pont-Sainte-Mayence (vv. 2060, 2095) mentions that Thomas Becket took the assumed name of *Crestiens* when he fled from Northampton in 1164.

In conclusion we wish to say a few words about the explanation of the Grail recently proposed by Albert Pauphilet in *Romania* LXVI (1940-41), 289-321; 481-504. He insists that the episode of the Grail question is the basic one. The trappings of the cup, lance, etc. were added to give dignity and moral effect. This release from bondage by the asking of a question or by the performing, or avoidance, of some physical act, is basic in the motif of the Release of the Dead. Pauphilet calls our attention to the story of Orpheus and Eurydice, and to two Breton tales published by Anatole Le Braz. He holds that the Grail Castle is the Land of the Dead. Of course, such a release is fated to be unfulfilled by a mortal.

We can not agree with Pauphilet in his emphasis upon this detail as the *central theme* of the *Conte del Graal*. His theory leaves too much of the essential *matière* on the periphery or completely outside the focus of the interpretation. He, like the "Celticists" gives the purpose of the story as an instruction book for a young knight. It is just possible, however, that the motif of Release of the Dead by a question properly asked could have been present in Chrétien's mind. After all, the Jews were spiritually dead and could be revived by their conversion to the New Covenant.

The Department of Romance Studies Digital Arts and Collaboration Lab at the University of North Carolina at Chapel Hill is proud to support the digitization of the North Carolina Studies in the Romance Languages and Literatures series.

www.ingramcontent.com/pod-product-compliance
Lightning Source LLC
Chambersburg PA
CBHW020423230426
43663CB00007BA/1287